the To&Through project

UCHICAGO **Consortium**
on School Research

I0167782

RESEARCH REPORT   OCTOBER 2017

The Educational Attainment of Chicago Public Schools Students: 2016

Jenny Nagaoka, Alex Seeskin, and Vanessa M. Coca

the To&Through project

The To&Through Project is a partnership between the University of Chicago's Urban Education Institute and the Network for College Success. The Project's mission is to use research, data, and professional learning to help more students get to and through high school and college:

- Research that illuminates what matters most for students' high school and college success
- Data that guides efforts to improve students' attainment of key milestones
- Professional Learning that helps translate research and data into improved practice

In collaboration with educators, policymakers, and communities, the To&Through Project aims to significantly increase the percentage of Chicago Public Schools freshmen who graduate from high school and go on to earn a college degree, and to share the learning from Chicago with education stakeholders across the country.

ACKNOWLEDGEMENTS

The authors gratefully acknowledge the many people who contributed to this report. The content of this report was shaped by valuable feedback provided by the To&Through advisory group and other members of the Chicago education community. UChicago Consortium Steering Committee members Gina Caneva, Nancy Chavez, Sarah Dickson, and Raquel Farmer-Hinton offered very thoughtful reviews as we finalized the narrative. We also appreciate the guidance on using Chicago Public Schools (CPS) data related to students with disabilities from Pal Baccellieri and Tamara West from the CPS Office of Diverse Learner Supports and Services. We thank members of UChicago Consortium's research review group, particularly Elaine Allensworth, Julia Gwynne, and Kylie Klein, as well as our external reviewers, Eliza Moeller and Will Torres, for their helpful feedback. UChicago Consortium's communications team, including Bronwyn McDaniel, Jessica Tansey, and Jessica Puller, were instrumental in the production of this report. Kaleen Healey and Valerie Michelman were authors on the first version of this report and shaped its content. We also thank Melissa Roderick and UChicago Consortium's post-secondary research team for providing the groundbreaking research base for this report.

This report was supported by the Crown Family Philanthropies. We thank them for their support and collaboration with this project. The UChicago Consortium greatly appreciates support from the Consortium Investor Council that funds critical work beyond the initial research: putting the research to work, refreshing the data archive, seeding new studies, and replicating previous studies. Members include: Brinson Family Foundation, CME Group Foundation, Crown Family Philanthropies, Lloyd A. Fry Foundation, Joyce Foundation, Lewis-Sebring Family Foundation, McCormick Foundation, McDougal Family Foundation, Osa Family Foundation, Polk Bros. Foundation, Spencer Foundation, Steans Family Foundation, and The Chicago Public Education Fund.

Cite as: Nagaoka, J., Seeskin, A., & Coca, V.M. (2017). *The educational attainment of Chicago Public Schools students: 2016.* Chicago, IL: University of Chicago Consortium on School Research.

This report was produced by the UChicago Consortium's publications and communications staff: Bronwyn McDaniel, Director of Outreach and Communication; Jessica Tansey, Communications Manager; and Jessica Puller, Communications Specialist.

Graphic Design: Jeff Hall Design
Photography: Eileen Ryan
Editing: Jessica Puller, Ann Linder, and Jessica Tansey

10.2017/500/jh.design@rcn.com

Introduction

The differences in opportunities based on educational attainment are growing increasingly stark. Of the 11.6 million jobs that have been added in the post-Great Recession economy, 99 percent have gone to workers with at least some college education.[1]

The importance of having a post-secondary credential to get a good job is well understood by policymakers and the public.[2] High school students also recognize the importance of educational attainment; aspiring to earn a post-secondary degree or certificate has become the norm. Among 2016 Chicago Public Schools (CPS) seniors, 85 percent reported that they planned to complete some form of post-secondary education, with 78 percent planning to complete at least a bachelor's degree,[3] a number that has remained virtually unchanged for the past 10 years.[4]

For over 10 years, CPS has seen its role as twofold: ensuring students exit high school with a diploma, while at the same time positioning graduates for success as they transition to the next stage of their education. The district has been a national leader in recognizing that a high school diploma is no longer sufficient for most jobs and, as a result, high schools must prepare students for post-secondary education and participation in the knowledge economy. CPS leaders have encouraged high schools to play a critical role in supporting first-generation college students in attaining their post-secondary aspirations. The district has strategically designed and implemented initiatives toward that goal, such as tracking students' FAFSA completion, providing college and career coaches to high schools, and making a post-secondary planning software tool available to all high students.

In 2006, in conjunction with CPS's post-secondary efforts, the UChicago Consortium on School Research's (UChicago Consortium) Post-Secondary Transition Project began examining patterns of post-secondary attainment.[5] Since 2014, the To&Through Project has built on previous Consortium research by tracking the annual progress of CPS students on the milestones to a post-secondary degree or certificate. By tracking key milestones, the To&Through Project seeks to highlight where the district has made progress and point to areas in need of greater attention.

Previous UChicago Consortium and To&Through reports on educational attainment have shown how CPS has made significant strides in helping more students reach key milestones. In this report, we note where progress has been uneven, with many CPS graduates

---

1   Carnevale, Jayasundera, & Gulish (2016).
2   For example, in the results of the Americans Value Post-secondary Education: The 2015 Gallup-Lumina Foundation Study of the American Public's Opinion on Higher Education (Gallup, Inc., 2016), 70 percent of adult respondents said it will be more important in the future to have a degree or professional certificate beyond high school to get a good job.

3   Numbers are based on responses to the 2016 *My Voice, My School* student survey responses from CPS seniors. In 2016, the high school response rate was 78 percent.
4   Roderick, Nagaoka, Allensworth, Stoker, Correa, & Coca (2006).
5   Roderick, Coca, & Nagaoka (2011); Roderick et al. (2006); Roderick, Nagaoka, Coca, & Moeller (2008); Roderick, Nagaoka, Coca, & Moeller (2009).

still struggling to meet their aspirations and complete a post-secondary degree or certificate. In particular, critical gaps in attainment remain between young men and young women in CPS; among students with different race/ethnicity; and among students with disabilities.

In Chapter 1 of this report, we provide our annual update on the percentage of CPS students reaching key milestones to and through high school and college. In Chapter 2, we examine leading indicators of reaching key milestones: Freshman OnTrack, ACT scores, high school GPA, college choice, and college persistence. In Chapter 3, we describe the progress of students by race/ethnicity, gender, and identified disability status. We conclude by providing implications for the findings in this report. This report serves as a companion to the information on individual high schools provided in the To&Through Online Tool.[6]

---

6 For additional information please see toandthrough.uchicago.edu/data

CHAPTER 1

Degree Attainment Index and Key Milestones that Matter

The UChicago Consortium has developed two metrics to estimate students' progression to and through high school and college (**see Figure 1**): the Direct Bachelor's Degree Attainment Index (Direct Bachelor's DAI) and the Bachelor's Degree Attainment Index (Bachelor's DAI).

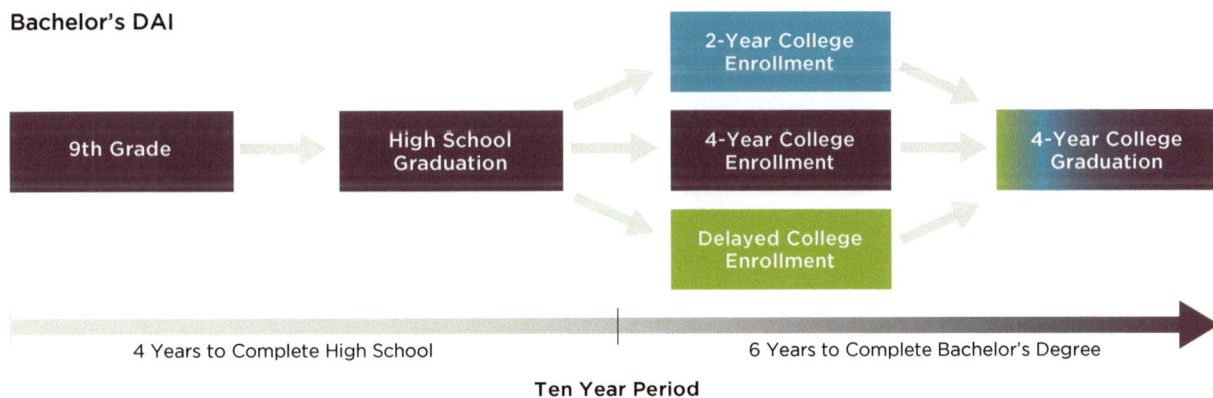

The Direct Bachelor's DAI estimates the percentage of students that will attain a bachelor's degree through a direct path over the course of 10 years: by graduating high school in four years, enrolling immediately in a four-year college, and earning a bachelor's degree within six years of graduating from high school. It only includes students who take a direct path through high school and college by making an immediate transition to a four-year college.

The Bachelor's DAI provides a better estimate of the total proportion of CPS ninth-graders who will earn a bachelor's degree within 10 years of beginning high school because, unlike the Direct Bachelor's DAI, it

encompasses all students who earn a bachelor's degree, not just those who enroll in a four-year college immediately after high school. It accounts for the different pathways students take to earning a bachelor's degree within six years of graduating from high school. It includes students who first enroll in a community college, students who delay entry into college, and students who enroll immediately in a four-year college.

Both the Direct Bachelor's DAI and the Bachelor's DAI are calculated using the most recent rates available for each milestone (high school graduation, four-year college enrollment, and four-year college graduation rates).

In this chapter, we describe the changes in the Direct Bachelor's DAI and the Bachelor's DAI for CPS students between 2006 and 2016.[7] We then provide trends for the three milestones that comprise the Direct Bachelor's DAI—high school graduation, college enrollment, and bachelor's degree completion—over time.

FIGURE 1

Direct Bachelor's DAI

9th Grade → High School Graduation → 4-Year College Enrollment → 4-Year College Graduation

Bachelor's DAI

9th Grade → High School Graduation → 2-Year College Enrollment / 4-Year College Enrollment / Delayed College Enrollment → 4-Year College Graduation

4 Years to Complete High School | 6 Years to Complete Bachelor's Degree

Ten Year Period

---

7   Throughout this report, the year refers to the spring of the school year so that 2016 refers to the 2015–16 school year.

Degree Attainment Index

Direct Bachelor's DAI

We estimate that 16 percent of 2016 ninth-graders, compared to 9 percent of 2006 ninth-graders, will take a direct path to a bachelor's degree by making an immediate transition after high school to enroll in a four-year college and graduate within six years (**Direct Bachelor's DAI; Table 1**). The 2016 Direct Bachelor's DAI is calculated by multiplying the 2016 high school graduation rate (74 percent) by the 2015 four-year college enrollment rate (44 percent) by the 2015 four-year college graduation rate (48 percent).[8] Nationally, the Direct Bachelor's DAI increased from 19 percent to 22 percent. Even with the increase in the national rate, in 10 years CPS has almost halved the gap with the nation in the Direct Bachelor's DAI, from 10 percentage points to 6 percentage points.

Bachelor's DAI

The 2016 Bachelor's DAI is 18 percent, 2 percent higher than the Direct Bachelor's DAI. That is, we estimate that 18 percent of 2016 ninth-graders will earn a bachelor's degree by 2026, a number unchanged from 2015. Indices such as the Bachelor's DAI are difficult to move year-to-year because they are based on multiple measures, and changes in one milestone have only a small effect on the final outcome if the other milestones do not change. However, CPS has shown dramatic improvements on the Bachelor's DAI since 2006, when the district first started focusing on post-secondary attainment; the 2016 Bachelor's DAI is a 7 percentage point increase above the 11 percent estimated for 2006 ninth-graders. We are unable to calculate a Bachelor's DAI for the nation because we lack data about the four-year college graduation rates for students who make an immediate transition to a two-year college and who delay entry to college. In the future, we intend to calculate an Associate's Degree Attainment Index for CPS that will focus on two-year college certificates and degrees.[9] **See Figure 2** for an illustration of 2016 Direct Bachelor's DAI and Bachelor's DAI.

High School Graduation

Over the past 10 years, high school graduation rates in CPS have shown remarkable improvement, increasing from 57 percent to 74 percent (**see Figure 3**). However, 2016 was the first year since 2010 that the graduation rate did not improve from the previous year. Still, because of the long-term improvement in the high school graduation rate, this represents more than 4,000 additional CPS high school graduates in 2016 than in 2006. The rising graduation rate was one of the

TABLE 1

Key Milestones and Degree Attainment Indices

	HS Graduation (Among First-Time Freshmen; Year of HS Graduation)		4-Year College Enrollment (Among HS Graduates)		4-year College Graduation (Among 4-Year Enrollees; Year of College Graduation)		Direct Bachelor's DAI		Bachelor's DAI	
	2006	2016	2006	2015	2009	2015	2006	2016	2006	2016
CPS	57%	74%	33%	44%	46%	48%	9%	16%	11%	18%
Nation	73%	83%	41%	44%	59%	59%	19%	22%	X	X

Note: The most recent data available for each rate are shown. High school graduation rate for the nation is from 2015. We are unable to calculate a Bachelor's DAI for the nation because we lack data about the four-year college graduation rates for students who make an immediate transition to a two-year college and who delay entry to college. Data and methods are described in Appendix A.

---

8 We use the most recent numbers available to calculate the 2016 Bachelor's and Direct Bachelor's DAI. 2015 is the most recent year for which we have college enrollment and gradua-tion data from the National Student Clearinghouse. The 2006 rate is based on rates that would have been available in 2006; that is, the 2006 high school graduation rate, the four-year college enrollment rate for 2006 graduates, and the four-year college graduation rate for students who graduated from high school in 2000 and completed college by 2006.

9 We use the National Student Clearinghouse data to deter-mine college enrollment and completion, but the data have incomplete information on certificate and associate's degree completion. To fill this gap, we are examining alternative data sources on community college completion for CPS graduates.

FIGURE 2

CPS Students' Path to Attaining a Bachelor's Degree Within 10 Years of Beginning High School

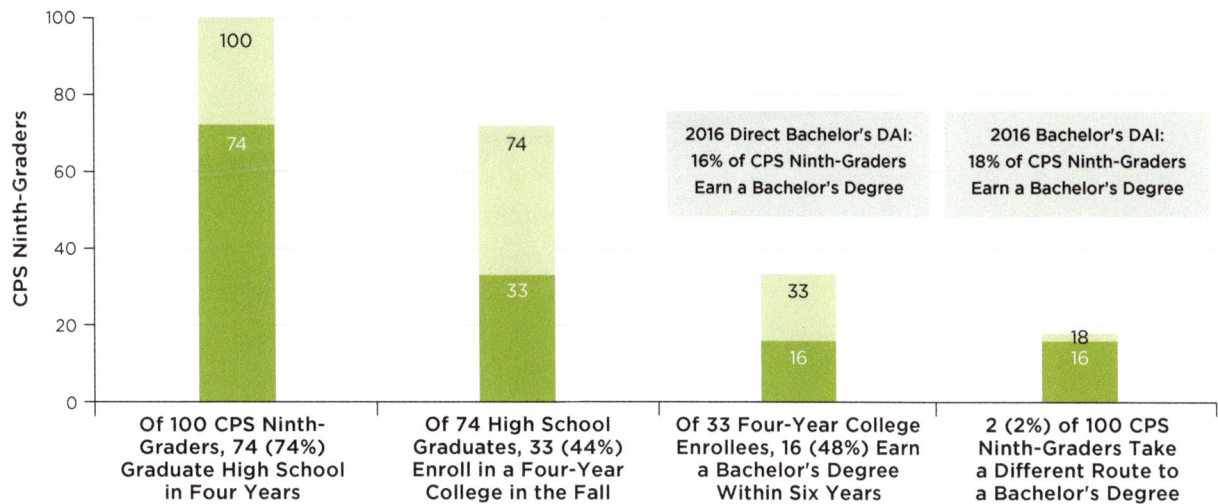

> **2016 Direct Bachelor's DAI:**
> 16% of CPS Ninth-Graders
> Earn a Bachelor's Degree

> **2016 Bachelor's DAI:**
> 18% of CPS Ninth-Graders
> Earn a Bachelor's Degree

| Of 100 CPS Ninth-Graders, 74 (74%) Graduate High School in Four Years | Of 74 High School Graduates, 33 (44%) Enroll in a Four-Year College in the Fall | Of 33 Four-Year College Enrollees, 16 (48%) Earn a Bachelor's Degree Within Six Years | 2 (2%) of 100 CPS Ninth-Graders Take a Different Route to a Bachelor's Degree |

Note: Data and methods are described in Appendix A.

FIGURE 3

CPS High School Graduation Rates Have Risen Dramatically Over the Last Decade

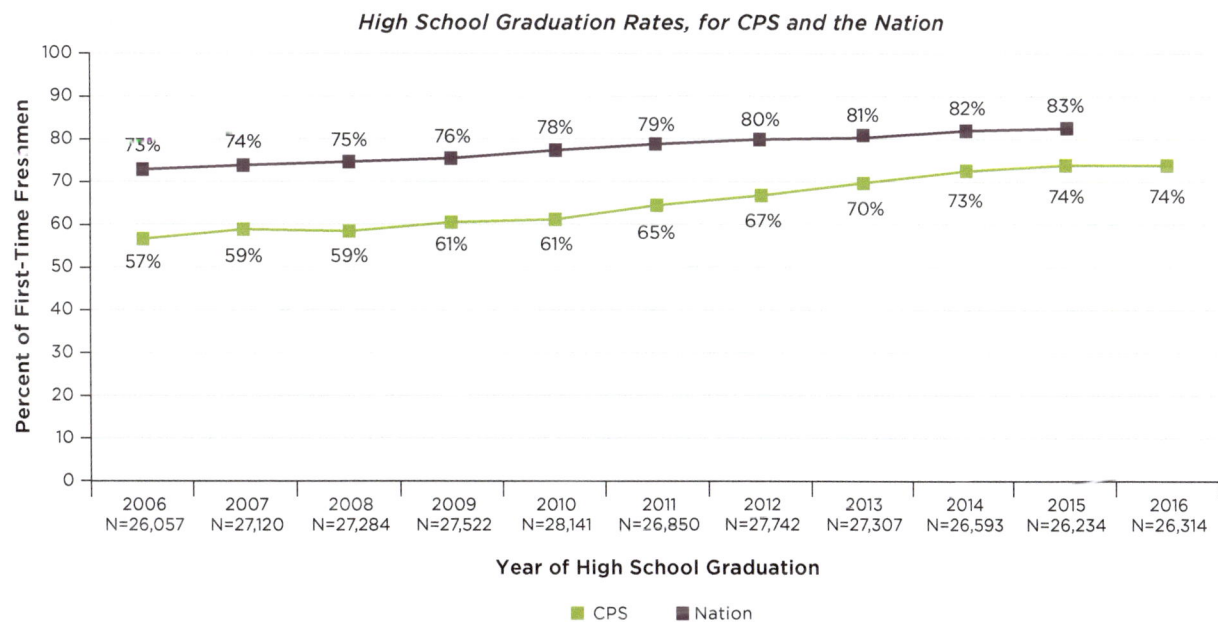

High School Graduation Rates, for CPS and the Nation

Year of High School Graduation										
2006 N=26,057	2007 N=27,120	2008 N=27,284	2009 N=27,522	2010 N=28,141	2011 N=26,850	2012 N=27,742	2013 N=27,307	2014 N=26,593	2015 N=26,234	2016 N=26,314

Nation: 73%, 74%, 75%, 76%, 78%, 79%, 80%, 81%, 82%, 83%

CPS: 57%, 59%, 59%, 61%, 61%, 65%, 67%, 70%, 73%, 74%, 74%

■ CPS ■ Nation

Note: Ns listed above refer to the number of students in an adjusted, first-time freshman cohort for each graduation year. Data and methods used to calculate high school graduation rates are described in Appendix A.

primary drivers in the improvement in the Bachelor's DAI. The increase in CPS's rate outpaced the increase in national public high school graduation rate, which increased from 73 percent in 2006 to 83 percent in 2015.[10] Although CPS's high school graduation rate lags behind the nation's overall graduation rate, it has nearly caught up to the national rate for low-income students: 76 percent.[11]

---

10 DePaoli, Balfanz, Bridgeland, Atwell, & Ingram (2017).

11 DePaoli et al. (2017).

College Enrollment

As CPS has been graduating thousands more high school students each year, concerns have surfaced about the graduates' level of preparation for college and the supports that are available for a growing number of students in the college enrollment process. However, even with rising high school graduation rates, more and more CPS graduates have made an immediate transition to college: 63 percent in 2015 vs. 49 percent in 2006. This increase was largely driven by growth in four-year college enrollment—44 percent in 2015 vs. 33 percent in 2006, an 11 percentage point increase (**Figure 4**).[12] Since 2006, two-year college enrollment rates have been relatively flat, going from 16 percent to 19 percent. The national college enrollment rates, in contrast to the overall trend in CPS, have remained relatively constant during this time period; national enrollment rates were 44 percent for four-year colleges and 68 percent for two- and four-year colleges combined in 2014. The October 2017 To&Through report entitled "Patterns of Two-Year and Four-Year College Enrollment Among Chicago Public School Graduates" provides a more in-depth analysis and discussion of college enrollment trends in CPS.[13]

Four-Year College Graduation

The four-year college graduation rate[14] for CPS graduates who immediately enrolled in four-year colleges has remained relatively constant over the past seven years (**see Figure 5**). Forty-six percent of students who graduated from CPS and enrolled in a four-year college in 2003 completed a bachelor's degree vs. 48 percent for 2009 college enrollees. The rate for 2009 enrollees was a slight dip from rates for 2007 and 2008 enrollees (48 percent vs. 50 percent); at this point, it is hard to determine if this is a temporary blip or the beginning of a downward trend. CPS's rate of four-year college graduation was well below the 60 percent rate seen nationally.[15]

FIGURE 4

College Enrollment Rates Have Increased, Especially at Four-Year Colleges

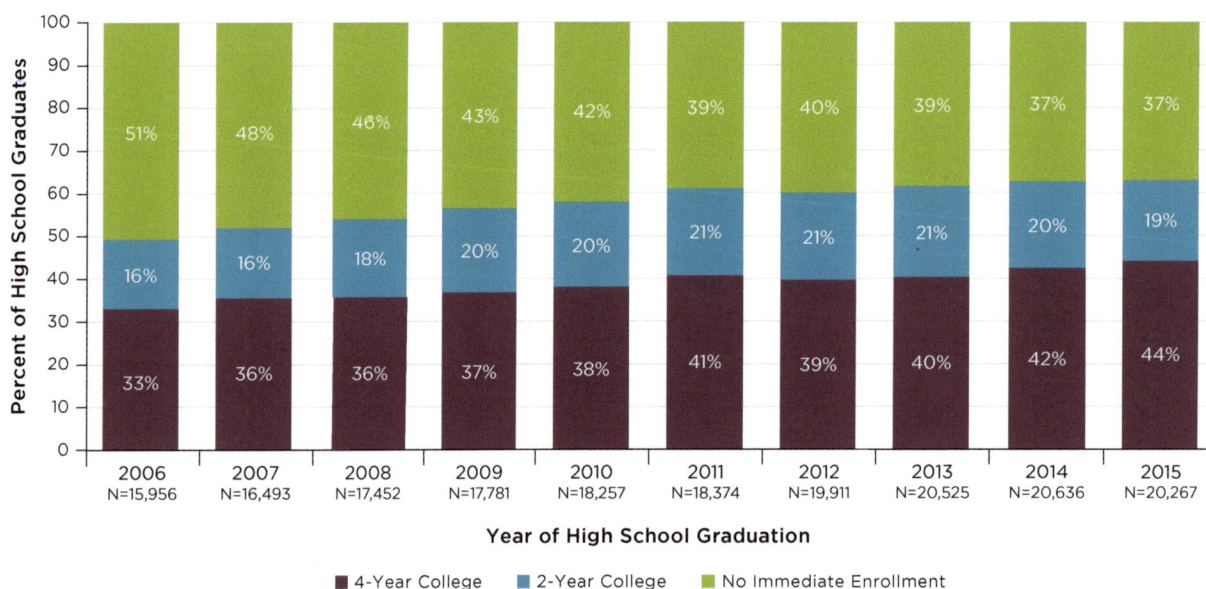

Note: Ns listed above refer to the number of the high school graduates for each year. Data and methods used to calculate college enrollment rates are described in Appendix A. Percentages may not add up to 100 due to rounding.

12 We use 2006 graduates to align with our bachelor's degree attainment figure.

13 Coca, Nagaoka, & Seeskin (2017).

14 The four-year college graduation rate is based on whether students completed a bachelor's degree within six years after they graduated from high school. Four-year college graduation rates are commonly measured after six years, and using this time frame allows for national comparisons.

15 U.S. Department of Education (2017).

Some students also take a less direct path to a bachelor's degree, so we also categorize students who did not make an immediate transition to a four-year college by whether they enrolled in a two-year college or did not enroll in college the fall after high school graduation. Students who made an immediate transition to a two-year college or who may have delayed entry to college were significantly less likely to earn a bachelor's degree; only 7 percent of students who started at a two-year college and 4 percent of students who did not make an immediate transition to college earned a bachelor's

degree within six years of graduating high school. However, it is important to note that these rates include students who enrolled in a two-year college with the intent of completing a certificate or associate's degree, and did not plan to complete a bachelor's degree.

Overall, with more students graduating high school and enrolling in four-year colleges, even a relatively constant four-year college graduation rate over the next six years means that roughly 2,100 more CPS alumni will earn a bachelor's degree each year than in 2006.

FIGURE 5

Four-Year College Graduation Rates Are Fairly Flat

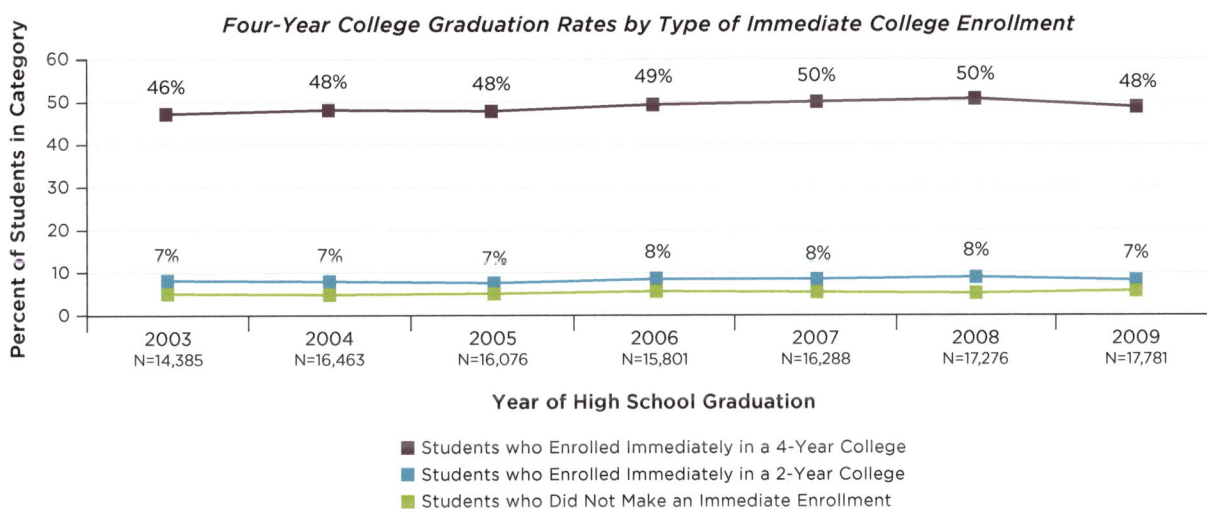

Four-Year College Graduation Rates by Type of Immediate College Enrollment

Year of High School Graduation

- ■ Students who Enrolled Immediately in a 4-Year College
- ■ Students who Enrolled Immediately in a 2-Year College
- ■ Students who Did Not Make an Immediate Enrollment

Note: Ns listed above refer to the adjusted number of high school graduates for each year. Data and methods used to calculate four-year college graduation rates are described in Appendix A.

CHAPTER 2

Leading Indicators of Key Milestones

Examining how many students are meeting key educational milestones is a critical way of assessing the progress of the district in helping its students meet their educational aspirations. Improvement in these key milestones can be informed by leading indicators that highlight to district leaders and practitioners how they might adjust their efforts to improve attainment rates. In this chapter, we take a closer look at five leading indicators of the attainment milestones: Freshman OnTrack,[16] composite ACT scores,[17] graduating core GPA,[18] college choice,[19] and college persistence.[20]

Prior Consortium research shows that students who are on-track at the end of their freshman year—having five or more credits and failing no more than one semester of a core course—are four times more likely to graduate from high school than students who are off-track.[21] Moreover, Freshman OnTrack is a better predictor of high school graduation than eighth-grade test scores, poverty, race/ethnicity, and gender combined.[22] GPAs and ACT scores are used in college admission decisions and shape students' access to college, particularly to more selective colleges, which tend to have higher institutional graduation rates. However, research has consistently found that high school GPA is a stronger predictor of each of the educational attainment milestones—high school graduation, college enrollment, and four-year college graduation rate—than test scores such as ACT.[23] It appears that the mechanism through which ACT scores shape college degree attainment is primarily through college admissions.[24]

College choice shapes a student's likelihood of graduating from a four-year college at least as much as academic credentials. Research has found that students with similar academic credentials (GPA and standardized test scores) have different likelihoods of attaining a degree depending on the institution they attend. The institutional graduation rate serves as a useful proxy for how students' college choices shape their own likelihood of graduating. In this chapter, we use the institutional graduation rates of the initial colleges where CPS graduates enrolled as a leading indicator of their likelihood of completion.

In order to complete a bachelor's degree, students must persist in a four-year college; persistence for two years in a four-year college is currently the best predictor we have of college completion.[25] Persistence rates allow us to report a post-college enrollment milestone for more recent cohorts of CPS graduates, since four-year college graduation rates can only be calculated for students who graduated from high school seven or more years before. Low persistence rates can reflect a myriad of struggles that students face for academic, financial, and social reasons.

---

16 Freshman OnTrack rate is the proportion of first-time ninth-graders who have earned five or more credits and have failed no more than one semester of a core course (English, math, science, and social studies) by the end of ninth-grade. It does not include summer courses or charter school students. See Appendix A for more details.

17 ACT score is the composite score students received when they took the ACT as part of the Prairie State Achievement Examination taken by all eleventh-graders in the State of Illinois. These statistics are likely underestimates of CPS students' performance submitted in college applications, because they do not reflect the higher scores that students who retake the exam may have submitted to colleges.

18 Core GPA is based on students' grades in English, math, science, and social studies. It does not include charter school students; see Appendix A for more details.

19 College choice is based on the institutional graduation rate of the colleges in which students enroll.

20 College persistence refers to the proportion of four-year college enrollees who enrolled immediately after high school graduation and have been continuously enrolled in one or more four-year institutions for two consecutive years

21 Allensworth & Easton (2005).

22 Allensworth (2013).

23 Bowen, Chingos, & McPherson (2009); Brookhart et al. (2016); Easton, Johnson, & Sartain (2017); Geiser & Santiclies (2007); Neild & Balfanz (2006); Roderick et al. (2006).

24 Roderick et al. (2006).

25 Accumulating at least 15 credits and having at least a 2.5 GPA are among indicators that higher education institutions and researchers have suggested using as predictors of college completion. However, those data are not currently available to the UChicago Consortium.

Freshman OnTrack

Freshman OnTrack rates have risen dramatically over the last decade as CPS started paying more attention to freshman year and ensuring more students passed their classes and stayed on-track (**see Figure 6**). Of the Class of 2006, only 64 percent of students were on-track at the end of their freshman year; of the Class of 2019, 88 percent were on-track, an increase of 24 percentage points.

Composite ACT Scores

With rising high school graduation rates across the nation and in Chicago, many have raised concerns about whether these high school diplomas reflect the same standards as in the past and whether graduates are college-ready.[26] Contrary to these concerns, qualifications have not declined among CPS graduates (**see Figure 7**).[27] As over 5,000 more CPS students took the ACT and graduated from high school in 2015 compared to 2006, the percentage of students that scored at least a composite ACT score of 21 increased from 23 percent to 33 percent.[28] However, many graduates still had low

ACT scores, which may limit access to many colleges that have a track record of high graduation rates.

Graduating GPAs

We have also seen an increase in CPS graduates' unweighted GPAs in core courses (English, math, science, and social studies). In particular, the percentage of students graduating with at least a 3.0 GPA increased from 21 percent to 32 percent between 2006 and 2015 (**see Figure 8**). We use 3.0 as a benchmark for college readiness because four-year college enrollees with a high school GPA of 3.0 or higher have at least a 50 percent probability of earning a bachelor's degree within six years.[29] At the other end of the spectrum, the percentage of students with less than a 2.0 GPA declined from 38 percent to 24 percent. It is important to note that, unlike the ACT scores, the information on GPAs does not include charter school students, who constituted 17 percent of 2015 graduates.[30] We do not know what effect the inclusion of this important population on the GPA rates would be.

FIGURE 6

Freshman OnTrack Rates Have Improved Over Time

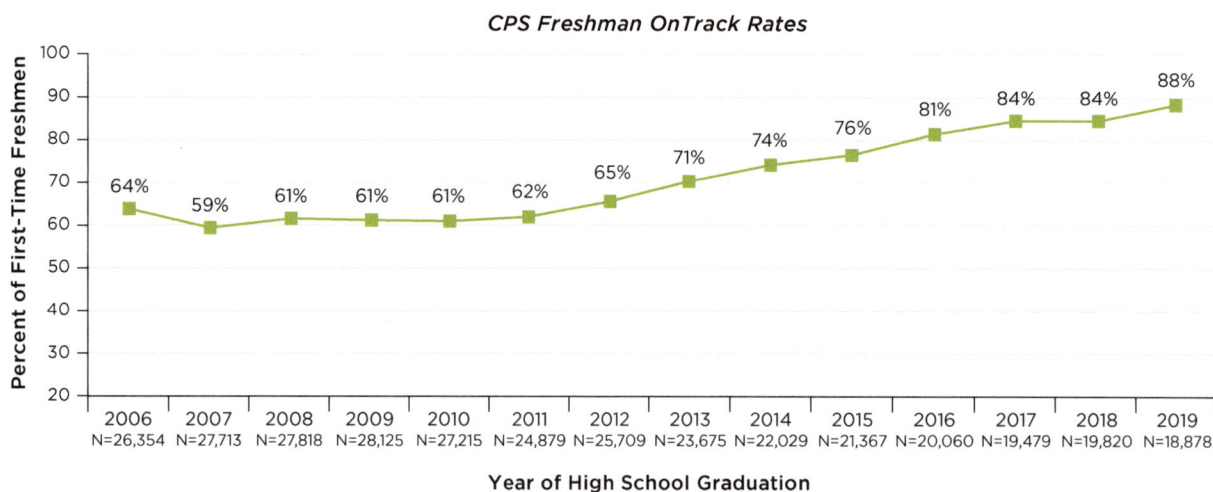

CPS Freshman OnTrack Rates

Year of High School Graduation	Percent
2006 (N=26,354)	64%
2007 (N=27,713)	59%
2008 (N=27,818)	61%
2009 (N=28,125)	61%
2010 (N=27,215)	61%
2011 (N=24,879)	62%
2012 (N=25,709)	65%
2013 (N=23,675)	71%
2014 (N=22,029)	74%
2015 (N=21,367)	76%
2016 (N=20,060)	81%
2017 (N=19,479)	84%
2018 (N=19,820)	84%
2019 (N=18,878)	88%

Note: Ns listed above refer to the number of the first-time freshmen for each year. Course grades for charter school students are not available. Ns and percentages do not include charter school graduates or students missing GPA information. Data and methods used to calculate GPA and to calculate freshman OnTrack rates are described in Appendix A.

26 Almond (2017); Camera (2016, April 27); Kamanetz (2016, April 27).

27 The ACT scores and GPAs are for 2015 graduates and correspond to the cohort used for the college enrollment rates.

28 The state of Illinois switched from using the ACT to the SAT for the accountability system in 2017.

29 Bowen et al. (2009); Roderick et al. (2008); Roderick, Holsapple, Clark, Kelley-Kemple, & Johnson (forthcoming).

30 Many CPS charter schools use different student information systems from the IMPACT system used by non-charter schools. Because each system varies in the way that it stores information about courses, credits, teachers, periods, grades, and other data, creating linkages across systems is difficult, and our data archive currently does not include records of charter school students' course performance.

FIGURE 7

ACT Scores Have Improved Over Time

Composite ACT

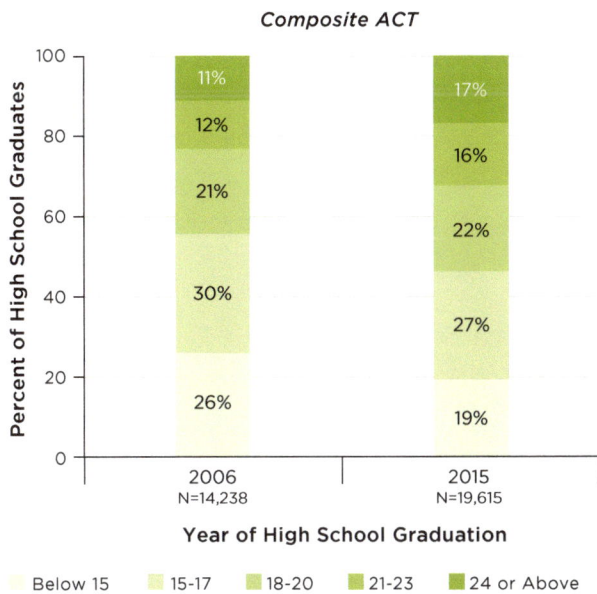

Note: Ns listed above refer to the number of high school graduates for each year. Ns and percentages do not include students missing ACT scores (1,718 students in 2006 and 652 students in 2015). Percentages may not add up to 100 due to rounding.

FIGURE 8

GPAs Have Improved Over Time

Cumulative GPA

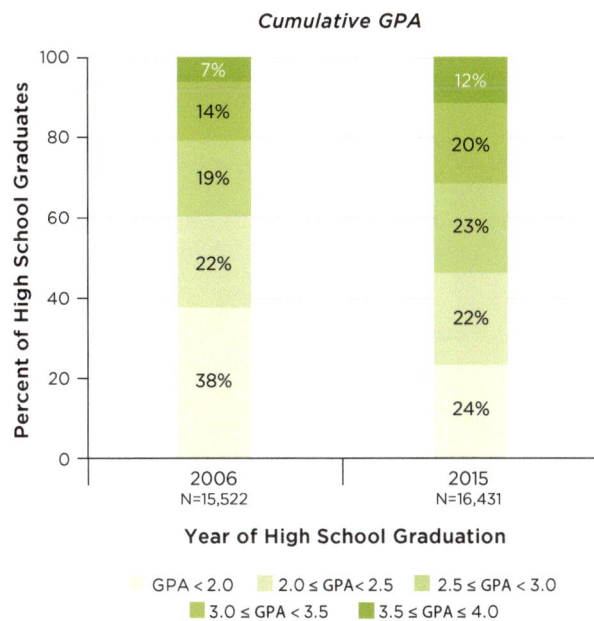

Note: Ns listed above refer to the number of high school graduates for each year. Ns and percentages do not include charter school graduates or students missing GPA information (434 students in 2006 and 3,836 students in 2015). Data and methods used to calculate GPA are described in Appendix A. Percentages may not add up to 100 due to rounding.

College Choice

Students' prospects for reaching the final milestone of college graduation is shaped not just by their GPAs and ACT scores, but also by the colleges they attend. Students with the same qualifications upon leaving high school are much more likely to graduate if they attend a college with a high institutional graduation rate.[31] Compared to 2006 four-year college enrollees, 2015 students were much more likely to enroll in colleges with institutional graduation rates of 50 percent or higher (58 percent in 2006 vs. 67 percent in 2015; **see Figure 9**). This change happened at the same time that almost 4,000 more graduates enrolled in four-year colleges (compared to 2006).

College Persistence

We use a two-year persistence rate, which we define as the proportion of four-year college enrollees who were continuously enrolled in a four-year college for two consecutive years. As shown in **Figure 10**, the persistence rates were largely stable between 2006 and 2009. However, starting with fall 2010 four-year college enrollees, we see a decline

FIGURE 9

2015 CPS Four-Year Enrollees Attended Institutions with Higher Graduation Rates

Six-Year Institutional Graduation Rates

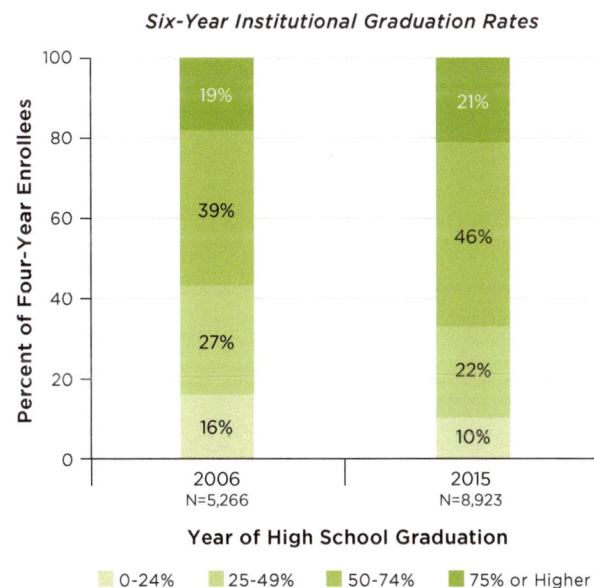

Note: Institutional graduation rates are from 2009. Ns listed above refer to the number of four-year college enrollees for each year. Ns and percentages do not include students attending post-secondary institutions missing information (45 students in 2006 and 65 students in 2015). Percentages may not add up to 100 due to rounding.

---

31 Roderick et al. (2006); Roderick et al. (forthcoming).

in two-year persistence rates. We do not yet know if this drop will translate into lower rates of bachelor's degree attainment. College completion depends on many factors, but the lower persistence rates suggest that there may be a drop in four-year college graduation rates in the coming years.

The rising Freshman OnTrack rates, ACT scores, and GPAs are hopeful signs that, as academic qualifications improve, we will continue to see increases in educational attainment. However, the decline in college persistence may indicate that, at least for the next few years, four-year college graduation rates may go down. It will take some time to determine whether there is, in fact, a decrease in CPS graduates' college graduation rates: 2016 high school graduates will not be included in our bachelor's degree attainment rates until 2021.

FIGURE 10

Rates of Persistence Among CPS Four-Year College Enrollees Have Fallen Since 2009

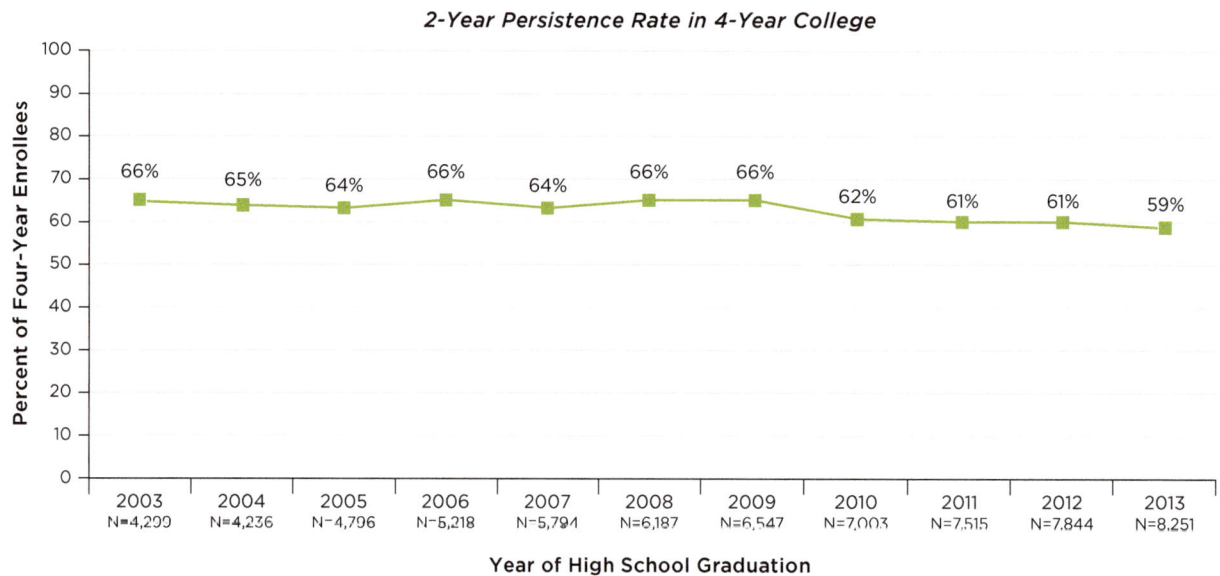

2-Year Persistence Rate in 4-Year College

Note: Ns listed above refer to the number of four-year college enrollees for each year. Data and methods used to calculate two-year persistence rates are described in Appendix A.

CHAPTER 3

Key Milestones by Student Subgroups

An enduring challenge for educators across the nation is ensuring that all students, regardless of gender, race/ethnicity, and identified disability, have the opportunity to attain the post-secondary credentials that are expected in the knowledge economy. As prior studies have shown, differences in attainment-related outcomes by gender, race/ethnicity, and disability status begin early and accumulate over time, ultimately culminating in sizeable differences in young adults' post-secondary outcomes.[32] Across the nation, young women are more likely to attain a bachelor's degree or higher than young men, rates that have remained unchanged over the last decade. While bachelor's degree attainment has increased across race/ethnicity groups, the rate of increase in attainment has grown more slowly for Black students than for Latino students, White students, or Asian students.[33] Young people with disabilities are much less likely to have bachelor's degrees than those without identified disabilities.[34] These persistent gaps in educational attainment are troubling, and have serious implications for the job prospects and future incomes of many CPS students.

In this chapter, we examine the patterns of attainment for CPS students by race/ethnicity and gender as they pertain to the three critical education milestones: high school graduation, four-year college enrollment, and four-year college graduation. We also explore academic preparation by examining GPAs and ACT composite scores. These data points and patterns can help schools and the district target supports for particular groups of students.

Finally, we explore the three critical milestones for students with identified disabilities, a group often overlooked in discussions of post-secondary access and success. Patterns revealed here can begin to shed light on how the high school-to-college transition is experienced for a group of students that made up 15 percent of incoming ninth-graders in the 2015–16 school year.

Race/Ethnicity and Gender

High School Graduation

While the findings from Chapter 2 show overall improvements in high school graduation rates and four-year college enrollment rates, there remains considerable variability in the percentage of students meeting critical milestones by race/ethnicity and gender.

Graduating from high school in four years was still a major hurdle for many CPS students, particularly Black students and Latino students. As shown in **Figure 11**, Black young men and Latino young men had the lowest rates of high school graduation in 2016 (59 percent and 73 percent respectively), followed by Black young women (71 percent), and White young men and Latina young women (both at 83 percent). White young women (89 percent), Asian young men (91 percent), and Asian young women (93 percent) all had high school graduation rates above the 2015 national rate of 83 percent. However, as **Figure 11** demonstrates, there have been significant improvements over the past decade for Black young men (18 points), Latino young men (22 points), and White young men (18 points).

One of the most striking patterns in 2016 high school graduation rates was the gender gaps within racial/ethnic groups. Young men have generally seen larger gains in their graduation rates over the past decade than young women. This has helped reduce the gender gap across racial/ethnic groups; for Black students from

---

32 Anderson, Kutash, & Duchnowski (2001); Bailey & Dynarski (2011); Buchmann, DiPrete, & McDaniel (2008); Cho (2007); DePaoli et al. (2017); DiPrete & Buchmann (2013); Fry (2011); Goldin, Katz, & Kuziemko (2006); Jacob (2002); Karen (2002); Reardon, Baker, & Klasik (2012); Robinson & Lubienski (2011).

33 U.S. Department of Education (2017).
34 U.S. Census Bureau (2016).

FIGURE 11

Gaps in CPS High School Graduation Rates by Gender and Race/Ethnicity Have Narrowed, but Are Still Large

High School Graduation

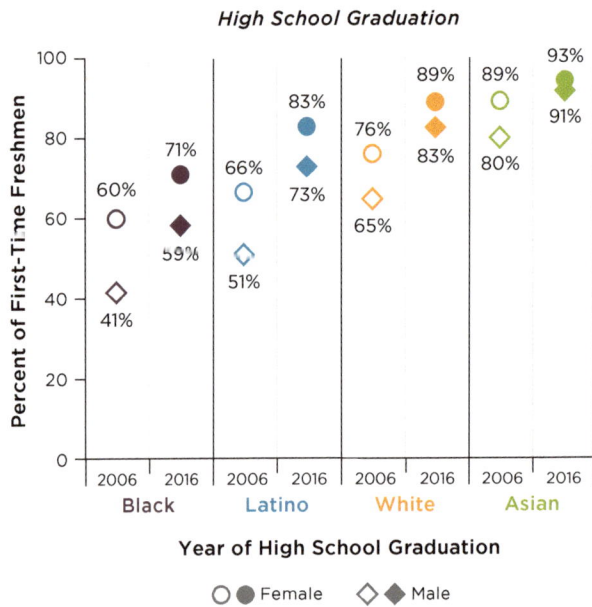

Note: Percentages do not include Native American students, Alaskan Native students, multiracial students, or students with missing racial/ethnic information (52 students in 2006 and 619 students in 2016).

FIGURE 12A

The Race/Ethnicity and Gender Gap in CPS Graduates' Two-Year Enrollment is Fairly Small

Two-Year College Enrollment

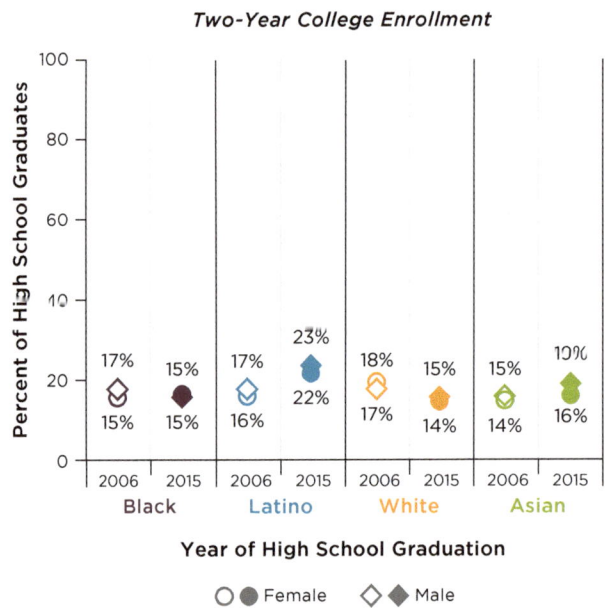

Note: Percentages do not include Native American students, Alaskan Native students, multiracial students, or students with missing racial/ethnic information (27 students in 2006 and 317 students in 2015).

19 to 12 percentage points, Latino students from 15 to 10 percentage points, White students from 11 to 6 percentage points, and Asian students from 9 to 2 percentage points. Nonetheless, the high school graduation rates suggest that Black students and Latino young men could especially benefit from additional supports.

Two-Year and Four-Year College Enrollment

Unlike high school graduation, male and female high school graduates of similar race/ethnicity enroll in two-year colleges at almost the same rates (**see Figure 12A**). With the exception of male and female Latino students, high school graduates enrolled at similar rates between 2006 and 2015 across racial/ethnic groups and across gender: around 17 percent. In 2015, 23 percent of Latino young men and 22 percent of Latina young women enrolled in two-year colleges, vs. 17 percent and 16 percent in 2006.

Among the students who graduated high school in 2015, there was more variability in rates of immediate entry into a four-year college. Specifically, Black students and Latino students had lower rates of four-year enrollment in comparison to their White and Asian counterparts, and male students had lower rates of four-year enrollment in comparison to female students. As shown in **Figure 12B**, Latino young men had the lowest rates of four-year enrollment, with only one-third enrolling in a four-year college directly after finishing high school—followed by Black young men (40 percent) and Latina young women (40 percent).[35]

Unlike high school graduation, though all groups have seen increases in four-year college enrollment rates over the last decade, the gender gap in four-year college enrollment rates has actually been increasing across racial/ethnic groups: for Black students (from 6 to 10 points), Latino students (from 5 to 7 points), White students (from

---

35 The National Student Clearinghouse estimates that less than 50 percent of undocumented four-year enrollees students are accounted for in the data they receive. This means that the

percentages of Latino college enrollees likely represent an undercount, though it is difficult to estimate how significant the undercount is.

The Race/Ethnicity and Gender Gap in CPS Graduates' Four-Year Enrollment is Increasing

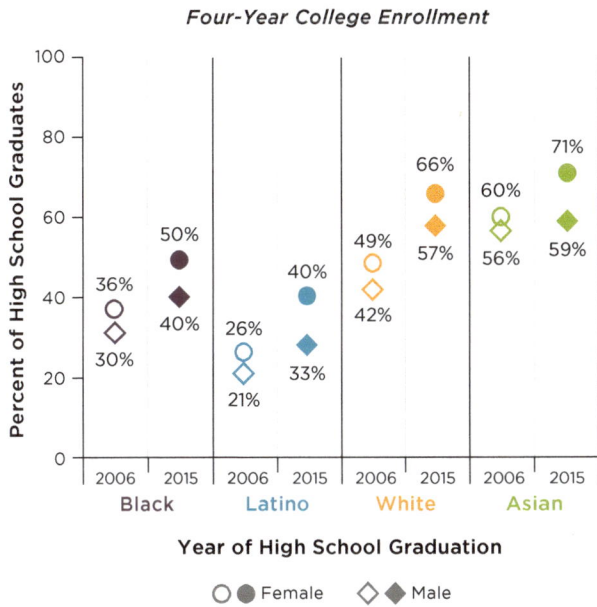

Four-Year College Enrollment

Note: Percentages do not include Native American students, Alaskan Native students, multiracial students, or students with missing racial/ethnic information (27 students in 2006 and 317 students in 2015).

FIGURE 13

Black and Latino College Enrollees Have Lower Rates of Bachelor's Degree Attainment than White and Asian Students

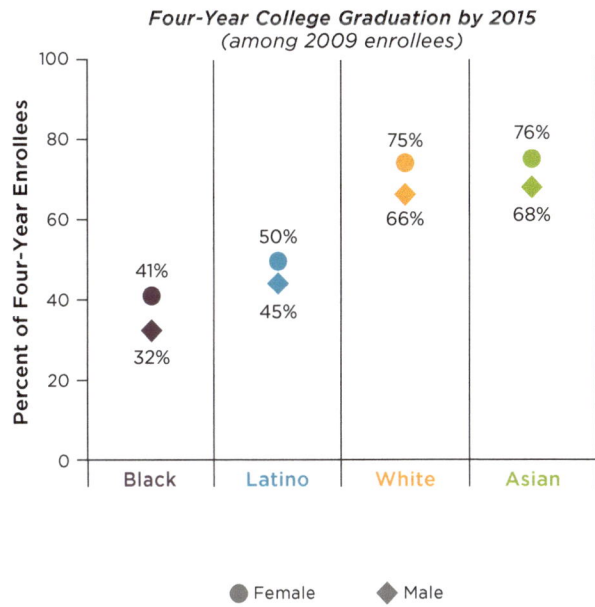

Four-Year College Graduation by 2015
(among 2009 enrollees)

Note: Percentages do not include Native American students, Alaskan Native students, multiracial students, or students with missing racial/ethnic information (12 students in 2009).

7 to 9 points), and Asian students (from 4 to 12 points). A more detailed examination of college enrollment rates, including enrollment in two-year colleges, can be found in the October 2017 To&Through report entitled *Patterns of Two-Year and Four-Year College Enrollment Rates Among Chicago Public School Graduates.*[36]

Four-Year College Graduation

Consistent with national trends on college completion, Black and Latino four-year college enrollees in Chicago had lower rates of bachelor's degree attainment compared to their White and Asian counterparts. The four-year college graduation rates for White and Asian young men and women outperformed the national rate of 59 percent. In addition, across racial/ethnic groups, young women who enrolled in a four-year college had higher rates of bachelor's degree attainment than their male counterparts. As shown in **Figure 13**, Black young men

were the least likely to complete a bachelor's degree within six years of enrolling in a four-year college (32 percent) in comparison to their female counterparts (41 percent) and those of different race/ethnicity. These patterns suggests that far more work is needed to support Black and Latino students in their college choices, as well as after they enter four-year institutions.

Direct Bachelor's and Bachelor's Degree Attainment Indices

The gaps in the three education milestones culminate in considerable gaps in Bachelor's DAI values (**see Table 2**). Relatively low high school graduation rates, four-year enrollment rates, and four-year college graduation rates mean that few Black and Latino ninth-graders were likely to earn a bachelor's degree within 10 years of starting high school. If these rates remain the same, only 8 out of 100 Black young men and 13 out

---

36 Coca et al. (2017).

of 100 Latino young men will earn a bachelor's degree within 10 years of starting high school. In stark contrast, 49 out of 100 White young women and 55 out of 100 Asian young women who enter the ninth grade will go on to earn a bachelor's degree.

Ideally, the patterns found in **Table 2** could serve as a way to help education stakeholders map out the scope of the challenge for closing the college completion gap. Using the index and the individual milestones within it can help educators identify where major challenges lie for various groups of students.

While the patterns in **Table 2** highlight significant gaps in education outcomes of students, they do not indicate what could be driving these gaps. Earlier we showed the distribution of ACT scores and GPAs for all CPS graduates. Next, we examine how academic qualifications vary by gender and race/ethnicity to better understand the patterns and potential factors that shape differences in educational attainment.

Composite ACT Scores

The differences in ACT scores by race/ethnicity are striking **(see Figure 14)**. While over one-half of White and Asian students, both male and female, scored at least the college-ready benchmark of 21, only around 20 percent of Black students and 30 percent of Latino students did. Low scores (at or below 17) were less common among White and Asian students, but over one-half of Black students and nearly one-half of Latino students scored in that range.

The other striking pattern in ACT scores is the lack of a gender gap within racial/ethnic groups. This is in sharp contrast to the consistent gender gap in reaching high school graduation, college enrollment, and college completion milestones. This suggests that gender gaps in reaching milestones are not being driven by ACT scores.

Graduating GPAs

In contrast to ACT scores, GPAs varied greatly by both racial/ethnic background and by gender **(see Figure 15)**. White and Asian students were more likely to graduate with a 3.0 GPA than Black or Latino students. However, 65 percent of White young women had at least a 3.0 GPA vs. 45 percent of White young men; and 72 percent of Asian young women vs. 58 percent of Asian young men have a GPA that high.

TABLE 2

Critical Milestones and DAI by Race/Ethnicity & Gender

	Number of First-Time Freshmen in 2016	2016 HS Graduation (Among First-Time Freshmen)		2015 4-Year Enrollment (Among HS Graduates)		2015 4-year College Graduation (Among 4-Year Enrollees)		Direct Bachelor's DAI	Bachelor's DAI
Total	27,936	74%	X	44%	X	48%	=	16%	18%
Black Females	5,630	71%	X	50%	X	41%	=	14%	16%
Black Males	5,425	59%	X	40%	X	32%	=	8%	8%
Latino Females	6,292	83%	X	40%	X	50%	=	17%	19%
Latino Males	6,594	73%	X	33%	X	45%	=	11%	13%
White Females	1,097	89%	X	66%	X	75%	=	44%	49%
White Males	1,164	83%	X	57%	X	66%	=	31%	34%
Asian Females	547	93%	X	71%	X	76%	=	50%	55%
Asian Males	563	91%	X	59%	X	68%	=	37%	44%

FIGURE 14

ACT Scores Differed Dramatically by Race/Ethnicity but Considerably Less By Gender

Composite ACT

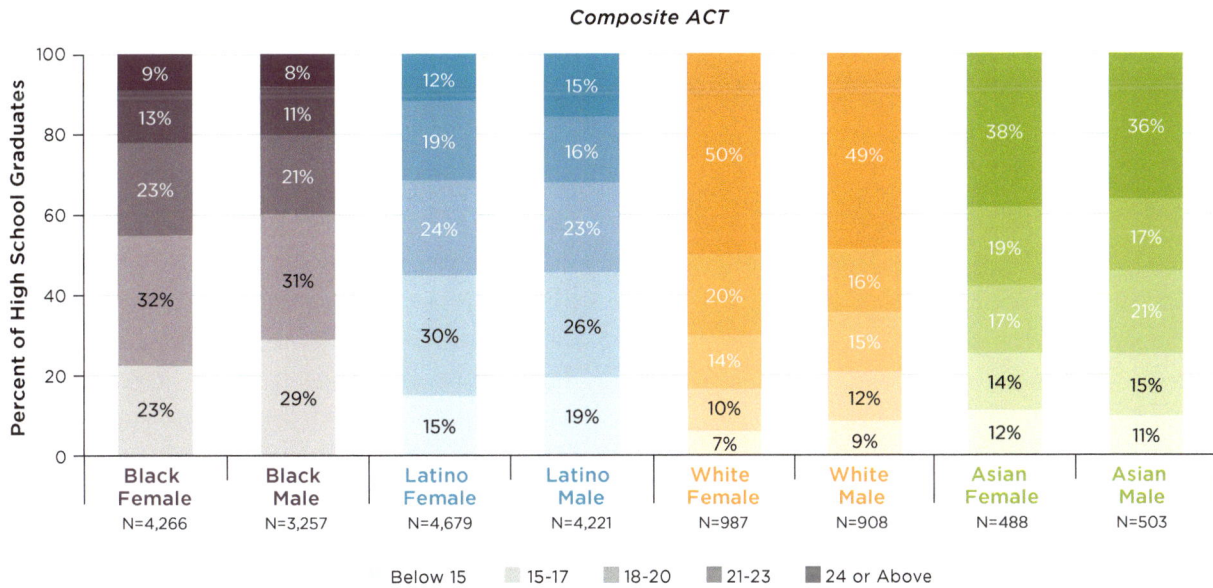

Legend: Below 15 | 15-17 | 18-20 | 21-23 | 24 or Above

Note: Ns listed above refer to the number of high school graduates for each group in 2015. Ns and percentages do not include students missing ACT scores (652 students in 2015). Percentages also do not include Native American students, Alaskan Native students, multiracial students or students with missing racial/ethnic information (317 students in 2015). Percentages may not add up to 100 due to rounding.

FIGURE 15

GPAs Differed Greatly by Race/Ethnicity and by Gender

Cumulative GPA

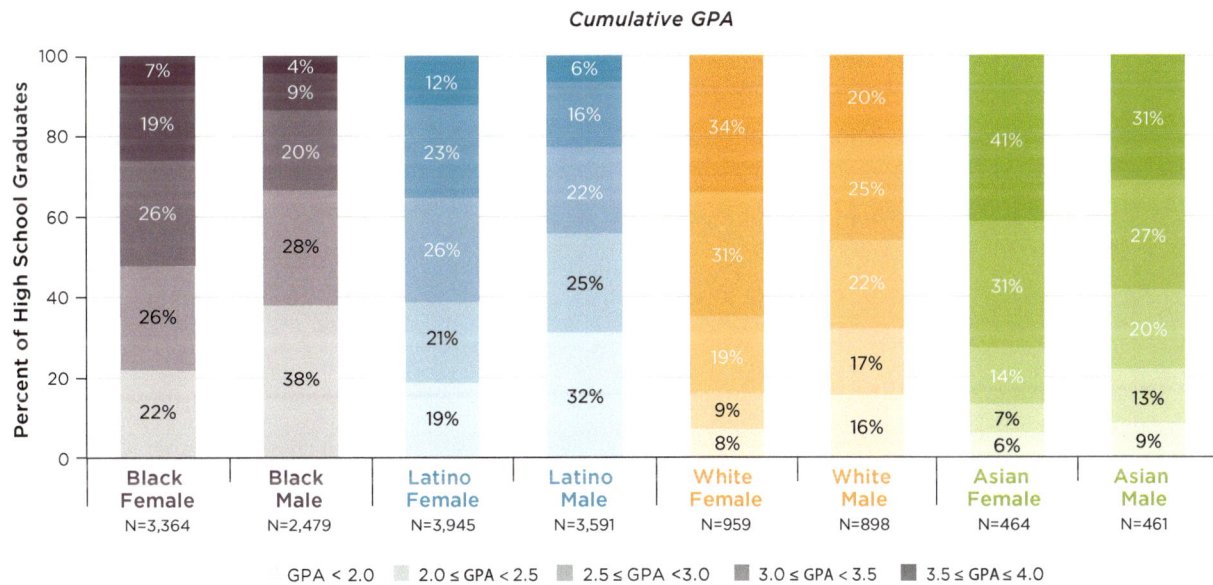

Legend: GPA < 2.0 | 2.0 ≤ GPA < 2.5 | 2.5 ≤ GPA < 3.0 | 3.0 ≤ GPA < 3.5 | 3.5 ≤ GPA ≤ 4.0

Note: Ns listed above refer to the number of high school graduates for 2015. Ns and percentages do not include charter school graduates or students missing GPA information (3,836 students in 2015). Percentages also do not include Native American students, Alaskan Native students, multiracial students or students with missing racial/ethnic information (317 students in 2015). Percentages may not add up to 100 due to rounding.

The story at the low end of GPAs is particularly disturbing: 38 percent of Black young men and 32 percent of Latino young men had GPAs below a 2.0. In contrast, 22 percent and 19 percent of their female counterparts had GPAs that low. It is also important to note that Black and Latino young men were much less likely to graduate from high school than their female classmates; there were over 1,000 fewer Black young men graduating and nearly 500 fewer Latino young men graduating. GPAs were a barrier to post-secondary success for both male and female graduates, but gaps point to very different experiences in high school, especially in light of the similarity in ACT scores. Finally, it is important to keep in mind that, unlike the information on ACT scores, charter school students were not included in reports on GPA[37] and Black students were disproportionately likely to attend charter schools.[38]

Students with Identified Disabilities

The 1975 Individuals with Disabilities Education Act (IDEA) mandates the provision of a free and appropriate public school education for eligible children and youth ages 3–21. In this report, we track the critical attainment milestones for students who received special education services, disaggregated by students' primary disability type (students with learning disabilities, physical disabilities, behavioral disabilities, and cognitive disabilities).[39] We disaggregated students by disability because, while students with disabilities are often treated as a single subgroup, their disability or disabilities vary widely in type and extent; as a result, their educational aspirations and outcomes may differ. This section is intended to highlight a critical subgroup of CPS students that have largely been omitted from previous Consortium reports on educational attainment.

In 2016, about 15 percent of incoming CPS freshmen qualified for special education services,[40] a slightly higher percentage than in 2006 (**see Table 3**). The 2016 CPS rate for students with disabilities mirrored the national rate in 2015.[41] Roughly two-thirds of 2016 CPS freshmen with disabilities were identified as having learning disabilities, and one-third of freshmen were identified as having another type of disability.

High School Graduation

For students with disabilities, we use a six-year high school graduation rate because, under IDEA, students with disabilities have the right to remain in high school

TABLE 3

Percentage of CPS Freshmen with Disabilities in 2007 and 2016

	2007 First-Time Freshmen 34,526		2016 First-Time Freshmen 27,936	
	Number	Percent	Number	Percent
Students with a Learning Disability	3,591	10.4%	2,794	10.0%
Students with a Physical Disability	470	0.7%	447	1.6%
Students with a Behavioral Disability	242	1.3%	251	0.9%
Students with a Cognitive Disability	691	2.0%	643	2.3%
CPS First-Time Freshmen with Disabilities (Total)	4,994	14.4%	4,135	14.8%

Note: Data and methods are described in Appendix A.

37 Many CPS charter schools use different student information systems from the IMPACT system used by non-charter schools. Because each system varies in the way that it stores information about courses, credits, teachers, periods, grades, and other data, creating linkages across systems is difficult, and our data archive currently does not include records of charter school students' course performance.

38 Twenty-eight percent of Black graduates attended charter schools.

39 Students may have been identified with other disabilities in addition to the primary disability categories used here to classify students. Learning disabilities include moderate and severe learning disabilities. Physical disabilities include students with visual, hearing, and other physical disabilities. We also include students with speech and language disabilities in this category because of the small number of high school students who have been identified with this disability. Behavioral disabilities include students with emotional and behavioral disorders. Cognitive disabilities include students who have been classified as mentally handicapped, autistic, having traumatic brain injury, or having severe or profound handicaps.

40 This does not include students with 504 plans.

41 Department of Education, National Center for Education Statistics (2017).

through age 21, even if they have completed the graduation requirements of their Individual Education Plans (IEPs).[42] Students with cognitive disabilities, in particular, are likely to take six years to leave high school with a diploma.

Overall, high school graduation rates varied by disability category, with students with behavioral disabilities graduating at much lower rates than other students (**see Figure 16**). In 2015, students with physical disabilities graduated at a slightly lower rate (71 percent) than CPS students overall (74 percent).[43] The six-year high school graduation rate for students with learning disabilities has increased by 18 percentage points since 2006; while the six-year high school graduation rate for students with behavioral disabilities has increased by 7 percentage points.[44] Six-year high school graduation rates for students with cognitive disabilities have not changed much over this time period.

Nationally in 2014, 66 percent of students who were served under IDEA between ages of 14 and 21 years old completed high school with a regular diploma, a rate

similar to CPS with the exception of students with behavioral disabilities and cognitive disabilities.

College Enrollment and Four-Year College Completion

Like their classmates, students with disabilities aspire to enroll in post-secondary education. Nationally, a little less than half of students with disabilities making their transition plans hoped to enroll in a two- or four-year college, and about 40 percent had the goal of enrolling in a vocational training program.[45] Although IDEA requires that high school students with disabilities have transition plans, states and school districts have been inconsistent in creating comprehensive and responsive services for students as they transition out of high school.[46] The transition to post-secondary education is further complicated by the great variation in the services and policies for students with disabilities across higher education institutions, as IDEA does not cover college students. Further, many college students

FIGURE 16

Overall, Students with Learning Disabilities Were Much More Likely to Graduate High School within Six Years in 2015 than in 2006

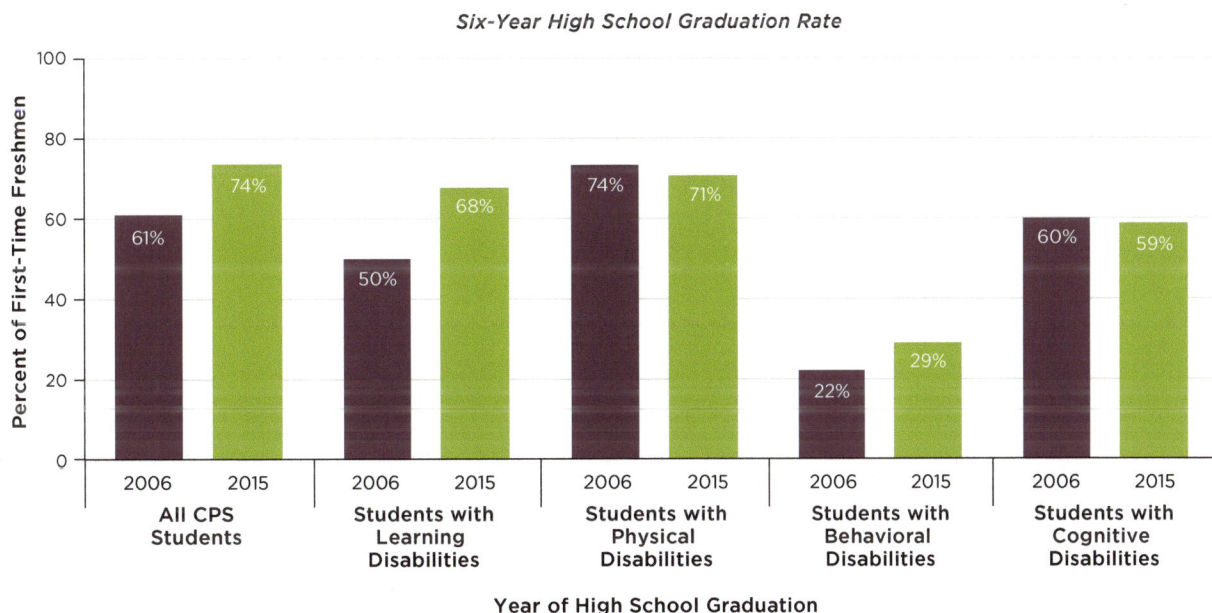

Six-Year High School Graduation Rate

Note: Data and methods used to calculate six-year high school graduation rates are described in Appendix A.

---

42 Using high school graduation after seven years, rather than six years, would increase the graduation rate by <1 percent. The six- and seven-year graduation rates for students without identified disabilities are identical.

43 The overall CPS graduation rate includes students with disabilities.

44 The 2015 graduation rate is for students who began high school in 2009, and the 2006 graduation rate is for students who began high school in 2000.

45 Cameto, Levine, & Wagner (2004).

46 Banks (2013); Johnson, Stodden, Emanuel, Luecking, & Mack (2002).

do not disclose their disability status and, as a result, they may not be receiving the services they did in high school. One study found that only 35 percent of students with disabilities informed their college of their status.[47]

College enrollment patterns among CPS high school graduates with disabilities changed dramatically between 2006 and 2015,[48] with the exception of students with physical disabilities (see Figure 17). Across all disability categories, 2015 high school graduates with disabilities were much more likely to enroll in four-year colleges than their counterparts in 2006. With the exception of graduates with physical disabilities, whose rates fell, graduates with disabilities were more likely to enroll in two-year colleges in 2015 than in 2006, as well. CPS 2015 high school graduates with learning disabilities were slightly more likely to enroll in a two-year college than a four-year college, and had an overall college enrollment rate around 42 percent. Students with physical disabilities showed a different pattern; they were twice as likely to enroll in a four-year college as a two-year college. About 43 percent of high school graduates with behavioral disabilities enrolled in college. However, because their high school graduation rate was only about 29 percent, this number reflects a small share of students who were identified as having behavioral disabilities in high school. Among high school graduates with cognitive disabilities, 29 percent enrolled in college, with about 17 percent enrolling in two-year colleges and 12 percent enrolling in four-year colleges.

Because the number of students with disabilities who enroll in four-year colleges is relatively small (125 in 2006, and 319 in 2015), we do not show their four-year college graduation rates broken down by disability category. Among 2003 four-year enrollees, 25 percent completed a bachelor's degree within six years. For 2009 four-year enrollees with disabilities, the rates were much higher: 34 percent of four-year enrollees completed a bachelor's within six years. Nationally, among 2005 high school graduates with disabilities who enrolled in a four-year college, 34 percent completed a bachelor's degree within eight years.[49] Given the proportion of students with disabilities who enroll in two-year colleges, the addition of two-year college certificate and degree completion data will be critical for being able to assess the extent to which they are making a successful transition post-high school after they complete their IEPs.

FIGURE 17

2015 HS Graduates with Disabilities Were Much More Likely to Enroll in College than 2006 HS Graduates

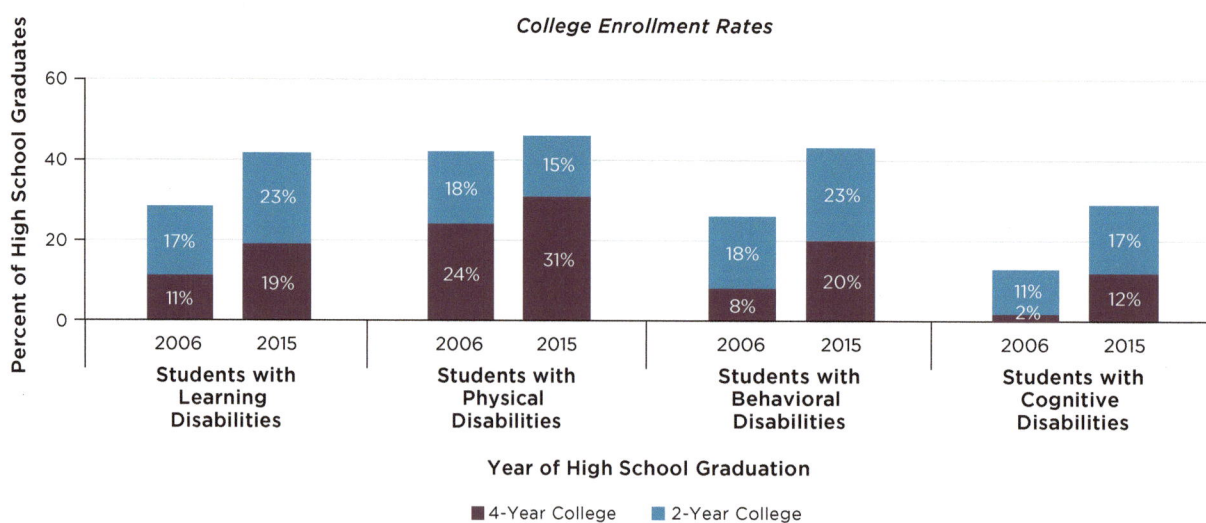

College Enrollment Rates

Note: Data and methods used to calculate college enrollment rates are described in Appendix A.

---

47 Newman & Madaus (2014).

48 2015 is the most recent year for which we have NSC data on college enrollment and college completion

49 Newmann & Madaus (2014).

CHAPTER 4

Interpretive Summary

Over the past 10 years, the Chicago Public Schools made great strides in improving the educational attainment of its students.

Compared to 2006, nearly 4,000 more CPS students graduated from high school in 2016, going from 57 percent of ninth-graders to 74 percent in 2016. This increase in high school graduation, coupled with an increase in four-year college enrollment rates—from 33 percent to 44 percent—means that CPS sent 3,500 more students to four-year colleges in 2015 than it did 10 years ago. According to an estimate based on the Bachelor's DAI, these improvements mean that approximately 2,100 more of today's CPS freshmen are likely to earn a bachelor's degree, compared to students who began high school 10 years ago.

The increases in educational attainment are much more than numbers; they represent life-changing opportunities for thousands of young people across the city. However, even with these improvements, there is still significant work to do across the milestones to ensure that all young people within Chicago, regardless of their race/ethnicity, gender, or disability status, are able to reach their educational aspirations and have the opportunity to reach their full potential in adulthood. This work cannot be done by the Chicago Public Schools alone; it will take families, communities, nonprofit organizations, civic leadership, and higher education to make it possible.

One of the key takeaways of this report is that young men, Black students, Latino students, and students with disabilities continue to graduate from high school, enroll in college, and graduate from four-year college at low rates. These rates are considerably lower than their White peers and Asian peers. Though these data are in line with national trends, and despite the significant progress the district has made over time, the gaps are a stark reminder that we need to make changes to our system to address these inequities and better serve all students.

The systematic differences in attainment by race/ethnicity and by gender suggest that the approach to addressing these inequitable outcomes will require more than interventions with individual students. It will require that the adults who intersect with young people, whether as teachers, family members, neighbors, youth workers, civic leaders, or researchers, also be reflective and interrogate how current practices and beliefs contribute to these inequities, and how they can be changed. Adults need to shift their teaching, support, and advising to better engage students in reaching key milestones toward their educational aspirations.

Over the past decade, the city has made significant progress across milestones, and within student subgroups, to provide greater access to opportunities in young adulthood. At the same time, the increasing shift towards a knowledge economy has made a college degree even more important for employment, earnings, and social mobility. Progress in Chicago over the next decade will depend on our ability to ensure that all of our city's young people are able to reach their full potential in adulthood and contribute to the future of our city.

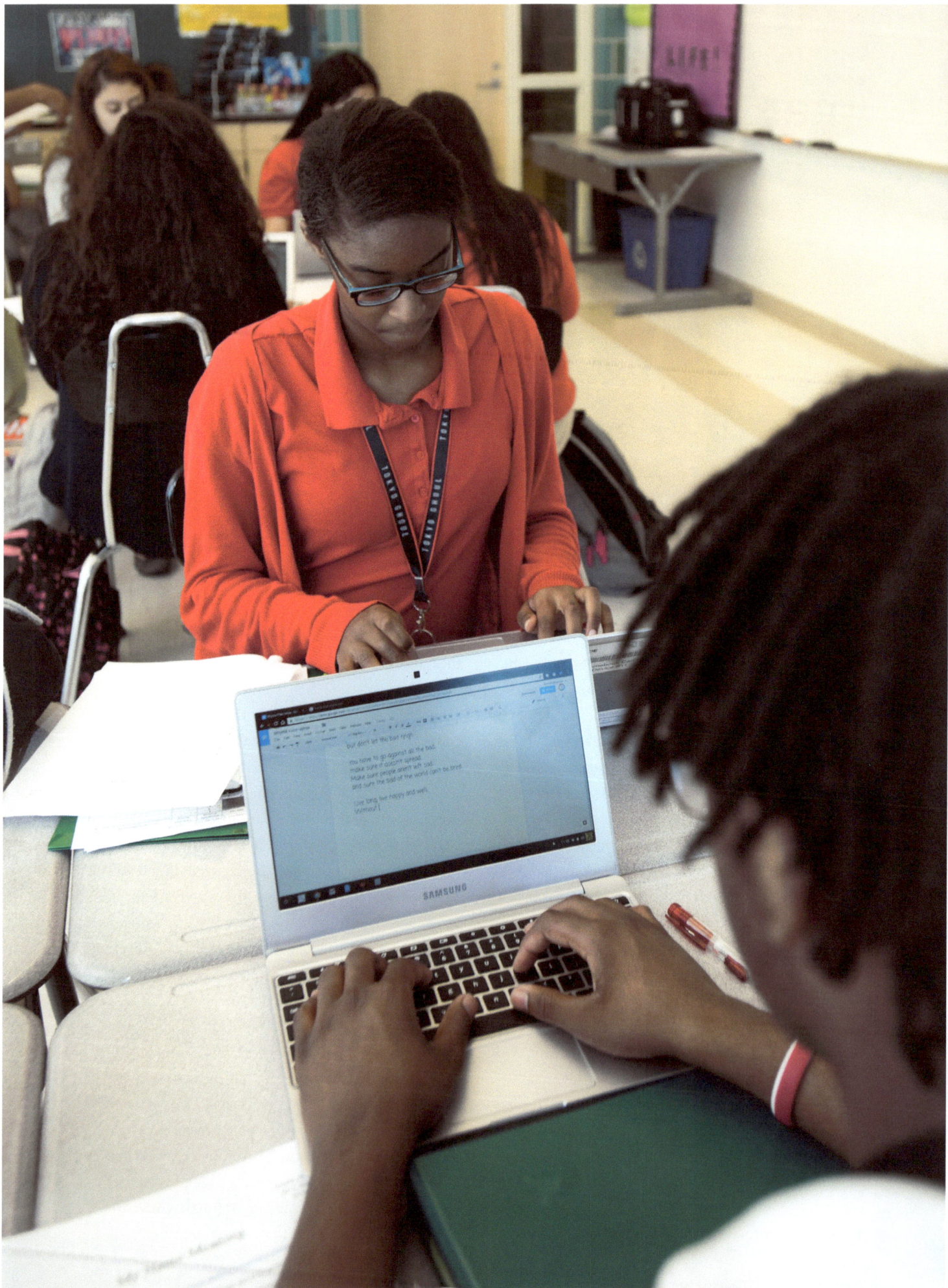

References

Allensworth, E.M. (2013)
The use of ninth-grade early warning indicators to improve Chicago schools. *Journal of Education for Students Placed at Risk (JESPAR), 18*(1), 68-83.

Allensworth, E.M., & Easton, J.Q. (2005)
The on-track indicator as a predictor of high school graduation. Chicago, IL: University of Chicago Consortium on Chicago School Research.

Almond, M. (2017)
Paper thin? Why all high school diplomas are not created equal. Washington, DC: Alliance for Excellent Education.

Anderson, J.A., Kutash, K., & Duchnowski, A.J. (2001)
A comparison of the academic progress of students with EBD and students with LD. *Journal of Emotional and Behavioral Disorders, 9*(2), 106-115.

Bailey, M.J., & Dynarski, S.M. (2011)
Gains and gaps: Changing inequality in U.S. college entry and completion. NBER Working Paper 17633. Cambridge, MA: National Bureau of Economic Research. Retrieved from http://www.nber.org/papers/w17633

Banks, J. (2013)
Barriers and supports to postsecondary transition. *Remedial and Special Education, 35*(1), 28-39.

Bowen, W.G., Chingos, M.M., & McPherson, M.S. (2009)
Crossing the finish line: Completing college at America's public universities. Princeton, NJ: Princeton University Press.

Brookhart, S., Guskey, T., Bowers, A.J., McMillan, J. Smith, L. Smith, J., & Welsh, M. (2016)
A century of grading research: Meaning and value in the most common educational measure. *Review of Educational Research, 86*(4), 803-848

Buchmann, C., DiPrete, T.A., & McDaniel, A. (2008)
Gender inequalities in education. *Annual Review of Sociology, 34,* 319-337.

Camera, L. (2016, April 27)
High school seniors aren't college-ready. *U.S. News & World Report.* Retrieved from: https://www.usnews.com/news/articles/2016-04-27/high-school-seniors-arent-college-ready-naep-data-show

Cameto, R., Levine, P., & Wagner, M. (2004)
Transition planning for students with disabilities. Menlo Park, CA: SRI International.

Carnevale, A.P., Jayasundera, T., & Gulish, A. (2016)
America's divided recovery: College haves and have-nots. Washington, DC: Georgetown University Center on Education and the Workforce.

Cho, D. (2007)
The role of high school performance in explaining women's rising college enrollment. *Economics of Education Review, 26*(4), 450-462.

Coca, V., Nagaoka, J., & Seeskin, A. (2017)
Patterns of two-year and four-year college enrollment among Chicago Public Schools graduates. Chicago, IL: University of Chicago Consortium on School Research.

DePaoli, J.L., Balfanz, R., Bridgeland, J., Atwell, M., & Ingram, E.S. (2017)
Building a grad nation: Progress and challenge in raising high school graduation rate. Baltimore, MD: Everyone Graduates Center.

DiPrete, T.A., & Buchmann, C. (2013)
The rise of women: The growing gender gap in education and what it means for American schools. New York, NY: Russell Sage Foundation.

Easton, J.Q., Johnson, E., & Sartain, L. (2017)
The predictive power of ninth-grade GPA. Chicago, IL: University of Chicago Consortium on School Research.

Fry, R. (2011)
Hispanic college enrollment spikes, narrowing gaps with other groups. Washington, DC: Pew Hispanic Center.

Gallup, Inc. (2016)
Americans value postsecondary education: The 2015 Gallup-Lumina Foundation Study of the American public's opinion on higher education. Washington, DC: Gallup, Inc. Retrieved from www.gallup.com/services/190583/americans-value-postsecondary-education-report.aspx

Geiser, S., & Santelices, M.V. (2007)
Validity of high school grades in predicting student success beyond the freshman year: High-school record vs. standardized tests as indicators of four-year college outcomes. Berkeley, CA: Center for Studies in Higher Education.

Goldin, C., Katz, L.F., & Kuziemko, I. (2006)
The homecoming of American college women: The reversal of the college gender gap. *The Journal of Economic Perspectives, 20*(4), 133-156.

Jacob, B.A. (2002)
Where the boys aren't: Non-cognitive skills, returns to school and the gender gap in higher education. *Economics of Education Review, 21*(6), 589-598.

Johnson, D.R., Stodden, R.A., Emanuel, E.J., Luecking, R., & Mack, M. (2002)
Current challenges facing secondary education and transition services: What research tells us. *Exceptional Children, 68*(4), 519-531.

Kamanetz, A. (2016, April 27)
Most high school seniors aren't college or career ready, says 'Nation's Report Card.' *NPR*. Retrieved from http://www.npr.org/sections/ed/2016/04/27/475628214/most-high-school-seniors-arent-college-or-career-ready-says-nations-report-card

Karen, D. (2002)
Changes in access to higher education in the United States: 1980-1992. *Sociology of Education, 75*(3), 191-210.

Neild, R.C., & Balfanz, R. (2006)
Unfulfilled promise: The dimensions and characteristics of Philadelphia's dropout crisis, 2000-05. Philadelphia, PA: Philadelphia Youth Transitions Collaborative.

Newman, L.A., & Madaus, J.W. (2014)
Reported accommodations and supports provided to secondary and postsecondary students with disabilities national perspective. *Career Development and Transition for Exceptional Individuals, 38*(3), 173-181.

Reardon, S.F., Baker, R., & Klasik, D. (2012)
Race, income, and enrollment patterns in highly selective colleges, 1982-2004. Stanford, CA: Center for Education Policy Analysis, Stanford University.

Robinson, J.P., & Lubienski, S.T. (2011)
The development of gender achievement gaps in mathematics and reading during elementary and middle school: Examining direct cognitive assessments and teacher ratings. *American Educational Research Journal, 48*(2), 268-302.

Roderick, M., Coca, V., & Nagaoka, J. (2011)
Potholes on the road to college: High school effects in shaping urban students' participation in college application, four-year college enrollment, and college match. *Sociology of Education, 84*(3), 178-211.

Roderick, M., Holsapple, M., Clark, K., Kelley-Kemple, T., & Johnson, D. (forthcoming)
From high school to the future: Delivering on the dream of college graduation. Chicago, IL: University of Chicago Consortium on School Research.

Roderick, M., Nagaoka, J., Allensworth, E., Stoker, G., Correa, M., & Coca, V. (2006)
From high school to the future: A first look at Chicago public school graduates: College enrollment, college preparation, and graduation from four-year colleges. Chicago, IL: University of Chicago Consortium on Chicago School Research.

Roderick, M., Nagaoka, J., Coca, V., & Moeller, E. (2008)
From high school to the future: Potholes on the road to college. Chicago, IL: University of Chicago Consortium on Chicago School Research.

Roderick, M., Nagaoka, J., Coca, V., & Moeller, E. (2009)
From high school to the future: Making hard work pay off. Chicago, IL: University of Chicago Consortium on Chicago School Research.

U.S. Census Bureau. (2016)
Educational attainment in the United States: 2015. Retrieved from: https://www.census.gov/content/dam/Census/library/publications/2016/demo/p20-578.pdf

U.S. Department of Education. (2017)
The condition of education 2017. Washington, DC: National Center for Education Statistics. Retrieved from https://nces.ed.gov/pubs2017/2017144.pdf

Appendix A
Data Sources and Definitions

Data Sources

Information on student demographics, ACT scores, course grades, and high school graduation is from CPS administrative records, which are shared with the UChicago Consortium through its Master Research Services agreement with the district. All data are available for charter school students, with the exception of course grades used to compute Freshman OnTrack rates and GPAs (see "GPA and Course Grades" on p.26 for details).

Data from the National Student Clearinghouse (NSC) are used for all college enrollment rates. The NSC houses records on enrollment and post-secondary credentials for colleges throughout the United States, and covers 98 percent of all post-secondary enrollments nationally. All of these data are available for charter school graduates.

Data Definitions

Throughout this report, the year refers to the spring of the school year; e.g. 2016 refers to the 2015–16 school year.

Key Milestones

High School Graduation

The four-year high school graduation rate is the proportion of students in an adjusted, first-time ninth-grade cohort who earned a regular high school diploma within four years, including the summer after their fourth year. Similarly, the six-year high school graduation rate (used in our analyses for students with identified disabilities) is the proportion of students in an adjusted, first-time ninth-grade cohort who earned a regular high school diploma within six years, including the summer after their sixth year. Students are considered a first-time ninth-grader if they had never before been enrolled in a CPS high school and if they either a) were actively enrolled as a ninth-grader on the 20th day of the school year or b) enrolled as a ninth-grader after the 20th day of the school

year and remained enrolled long enough to receive course grades. Charter schools GPA data is unavailable for our analyses at this time (see "GPA and Course Grades" on p.26) and so students who enrolled in a charter school after the 20th day are included in the first-time ninth-grade cohort, even though we do not know if they remained enrolled long enough to receive grades. High schools include programs CPS developed for students who had not passed the eighth-grade test benchmarks and were aged 15 or more (e.g., transition centers, academic preparatory centers, achievement academies).

Students who transferred into CPS after ninth grade are included in the cohort that corresponds to their grade and are assigned to the first CPS high school they enrolled in. Ungraded special education students, students whose first CPS enrollment was at an alternative school, and students who permanently transferred out of CPS (whether the transfer was verified or not) are not included in first-time freshmen cohorts. Students who earned a diploma from an alternative school or program are counted as non-graduates.

College Enrollment

For most of this report, college enrollment rate is the proportion of high school graduates who enrolled in a post-secondary institution (which participates in the NSC) in the *fall following high school graduation*. Graduates who enroll in primarily baccalaureate degree-granting institutions are considered four-year enrollees; graduates who enroll in institutions that primarily grant associate's degrees or certificates are considered two-year college enrollees. Off-cycle graduates are counted as graduates in the school year in which they graduated. Graduates are not counted as college enrollees either if they enroll in colleges that do not report enrollment data to the NSC, or if they request that their college not share their data with the NSC.

Individual schools may have better data on their graduates' college enrollment. The NSC relies on a matching algorithm to pair data provided by CPS on their graduates with data provided by colleges. This algorithm may produce different results using data provided by schools, which may be more current than the data given by CPS. Additionally, schools may have other evidence (e.g., course schedules or transcripts) of their graduates' college enrollment.

College Graduation Rate from Four-Year Colleges

The college graduation rate is the proportion of immediate four-year enrollees who earned a bachelor's degree from a four-year college within six years. Data on college graduation comes from the NSC. Students who earn a bachelor's degree from a different four-year college than where they first enrolled after high school are counted as four-year college graduates. Students who enroll in a four-year college that does not provide graduation records to the NSC in the fourth through sixth years after high school graduation are not included in these rates, as we are unable to determine if they earned a bachelor's degree.

Degree Attainment Indices

Direct Bachelor's Degree Attainment Index

The Direct Bachelor's Degree Attainment Index (Direct Bachelor's DAI) is the product of the most recent rates available for high school graduation, four-year college enrollment, and four-year college graduation (**see definitions of these terms on p.25-26**). It provides an estimate of the percentage of ninth-graders who will take a straightforward route to a bachelor's degree within 10 years of beginning high school. The Direct Bachelor's Degree Attainment Index is not the rate at which any single cohort of CPS ninth-graders obtains a bachelor's degree; rather it uses the most recent numbers for the three milestones to give a picture of the current state of the district.

Bachelor's Degree Attainment Index

The Bachelor's Degree Attainment Index (Bachelor's DAI) provides a better estimate of the proportion of ninth-graders who will earn a bachelor's degree within 10 years of beginning high school because it accounts for students who take alternative routes to a bachelor's degree, either by delaying college entry or by first enroll-ing in a two-year college. While the Direct Bachelor's DAI only includes enrollment and graduation rates for four-year college enrollees, the Bachelor's DAI uses the enrollment and four-year college graduation rates for two additional groups of CPS graduates: those who enroll in a two-year college and those who delay college enrollment.

Leading Indicators

Freshman OnTrack Rate

Freshman OnTrack rate is the proportion of first-time ninth-graders who have earned five or more credits and have failed no more than one semester of a core course (English, math, science, and social studies) by the end of ninth grade. On-track status was not calculated for freshmen who were enrolled only for one semester during the year, and does not include summer course-work. Course grades for charter school students are not available (**see GPA and Course Grades, below**), so we are unable to calculate on-track rates for charter schools. Charter school students constituted 28 percent of first-time freshmen in the class of 2016 cohort.

ACT Composite Score

ACT composite score is the composite score students received when they took the ACT as part of the Prairie State Achievement Examination taken by all eleventh-graders in the state of Illinois. These statistics are likely underestimates of CPS students' performance submitted in college applications because they do not reflect the higher scores that students who retake the exam may have submitted to colleges. These statistics differ from those published by CPS because they reflect the scores of graduates and not the scores of all students who take the ACT.

GPA and Course Grades

GPA is the cumulative, unweighted average of grades received in core courses (English, math, science, and social studies) at graduation. Only GPAs based on four or more semester credits are included.

Many CPS charter schools use different student information systems from the IMPACT system used by non-charter schools. Because each system varies in the way that it stores information about courses, credits, teachers, periods, grades, and other data, creating linkages across systems is a difficult, and our data archive currently does not include records of charter school students' course performance. We are therefore unable to include charter school students in GPA analyses. Charter school students constituted 17 percent of 2015 graduates.

College Choice

College choice is based on the institutional graduation rate of the colleges in which students enroll, and is categorized by quartiles. Institutional graduation rate is based on the proportion of full-time, first-time college freshmen who earned a bachelor's degree within six years. Data on institutional graduation rates come from the Integrated Postsecondary Education Data System (IPEDS), which is collected by the U.S. Department of Education's National Center for Education Statistics.

College Persistence

College persistence is the proportion of four-year college enrollees who enrolled immediately after high school graduation and have been continuously enrolled in one or more four-year institutions for two consecutive years. Like the college graduation rate, students who enrolled in a college that does not provide graduation records to the NSC in the fourth through sixth years after high school graduation are not included in persistence rates.

ABOUT THE AUTHORS

JENNY NAGAOKA is the Deputy Director of the UChicago Consortium, where she has conducted research for nearly 20 years. Her research interests focus on policy and practice in urban education reform, particularly using data to connect research and practice and examining the school environments and instructional practices that promote college readiness and success. She has co-authored numerous journal articles and reports, including studies of college readiness, noncognitive factors, the transition from high school to post-secondary education, and authentic intellectual instruction. She is the lead researcher on the To&Through Project, a project that provides educators, policymakers, and families with research, data, and training on the milestones that matter most for college success. Nagaoka is the lead author of *Foundations for Young Adult Success: A Developmental Framework* (2015), which draws on research and practice evidence to build a coherent framework of the foundational factors for young adult success, and investigates their development from early childhood through young adulthood and how they can be supported through developmental experiences and relationships.

Nagaoka received her BA from Macalester College and her master's degree in public policy from the Irving B. Harris School of Public Policy at the University of Chicago.

ALEX SEESKIN is the Chief Strategy Officer at the University of Chicago Urban Education Institute (UEI), where he is responsible for guiding strategy for organizing and leading high-priority work across and within UEI's units. Seeskin also leads the To&Through Project (toandthrough. uchicago.edu), which aims to empower educators and families with the research, data, and resources they need to move more students to and through high school and college. Previously, he served as the Director of Strategy of UChicago Charter and as a resident at UChicago Impact.

Prior to coming to UEI, Seeskin taught high school English in Chicago Public Schools for seven years, serving as the English department chair at Lake View High School from 2008–12. Seeskin earned a BS in communications from Northwestern University and an EdLD from Harvard University.

VANESSA M. COCA is an independent research consultant for the UChicago Consortium with extensive experience conducting research on post-secondary transitions of public school students in Chicago and New York City. As an Institute of Education Sciences (IES) pre-doctoral research fellow at the Research Alliance for New York City Schools—a research center housed at New York University (NYU)—Coca developed a massive longitudinal database to track the college transitions of all New York City (NYC) public school students and supported the NYC Partnership for College Readiness and Success, a research-practitioner partnership between the City University of New York City, the NYC Department of Education, and the Research Alliance. She is the lead author of *New York City Goes to College: A First Look at Patterns of College Enrollment, Persistence, and Degree Attainment for NYC Students* (2014), the Alliance's inaugural report that examined trends in college enrollment, persistence, and completion utilizing this longitudinal database.

Prior to her work at the Alliance, Coca worked as a Senior Research Analyst at the UChicago Consortium as part of the Chicago post-secondary transitions project, where she contributed to a series of highly regarded reports on CPS students' transitions to college. Coca received a BA and a master's degree in public policy from the University of Chicago. She is currently a doctoral candidate in the sociology of education program at the Steinhardt School of Culture, Education, and Human Development at NYU.

This report reflects the interpretation of the authors. Although the UChicago Consortium's Steering Committee provided technical advice, no formal endorsement by these individuals, organizations, or the full Consortium should be assumed.

9780997507348